is a gateway

Jane Spiro

Jane Spiro

Oversteps Books

For Lynn and Jon
with love and
in celebration of all
our past and futures

First published in 2018 by

Oversteps Books Ltd
6 Halwell House
South Pool
Nr Kingsbridge
Devon
TQ7 2RX
UK

www.overstepsbooks.com

ISBN 978-1-906856-77-9

Printed in Great Britain by imprint digital, Devon

a poetry journey in four seasons

where we start
summer's lease
swimming deeper
a white in us

Acknowledgements

With thanks for the reprinting of poems published in: *Orbis, The Journal* and *Rialto*; in anthologies with *Kent and Sussex poetry competition*, *Two Rivers*, *Back Room Poets* and *Moor Poets 3;* and photo-poetry exhibitions with Michael Carter and John Daniel.
Thanks to the following venues where some of the poems were performed: the Albion Beatnik, Oxford; the Jazz café Nottingham; Exeter Poetry festival; Ways with Words Dartington; and the Oxford Brookes Poetry Centre.

In addition, thanks to dear friends with whom I discovered Hungary: Judit Zerkowitz, Erika Varsany, Erika Kristof and Crystal Ashley; and to Noriko who conducted the tea ceremony in Tottori, Japan.

Poems are also dedicated to the life of my father, Martin (Miecik) Spiro (1922 – 2016), and my lifelong friend-in-poetry, Joanna Seldon (1954 – 2016).

Contents

Painting eggs

This white oval is where we start.

You take its life carefully between thumb and index,
pencil in the patterns you desire,
each round mirroring another,

the symmetry of a snowflake,
tight grids of a honeycomb,
markings of butterfly wings.

You start with an emptiness
sealed with wax,
a hope of colour –
dip into deep dyes, cautious to intense,
yellow to black, blind each layer
with wax dripped from a tiny pipe,

pause between layers for drying,
for patience, lengthening time
by a Ukrainian fire –

and when its colours have soaked deep
you wipe the wax so it falls reluctantly,
shuffling off its finished shell

and the egg emerges
jewel- bright, its turtle-back
an astonishment of colour

like the shock of birth.

Learning about grass

This is a new way of falling,
on purpose, because the landing
is giving and green,
comes up into your hair.
leaves green messages
on your sleeves and stuck
into the red weave of your hat.

It's like a dream
that takes you on a turnaround journey
sky/grass/sky on and off in light/dark stripes,
and the grass is all damp-delicious
smelling like the outdoors,
what it is to hear the squelch of mud,
to roll down the hill again
knowing it will leave patches of grass,
memories, clinging to your coat
and stuck to your hat like a winner's flag.

Learning to be four

He has learned to eat an olive
separating the flesh in his mouth
spitting out the stone.

He has learned the weight of a plate
holding his hands out to collect it
with its slices of peach.

He has learned the meaning of
new year 'revolutions' and his are:
to play games and to play more games.

He has learned to tap the computer
into life and move the arrow
so it conjures sea-monsters and tarantulas.

He has learned precisely
the ingredients of spam musubi –
spam and seaweed and rice.

He can run like a speedboat
with burring engine
and tiny pumping arms.

He invents a game with Mr. Leaves
and Mr Chairs and Mr Clouds
and says *they are all my brothers.*

He circles the new year sparkler
and says, from a memory he has found,
it's a work of genius.

All this in not five years
in which time we have grown hardly at all
forgetting how much can come from nothing,
and how soon.

Playing alone

She is playing alone, they said.
We are worried she has chosen
to avoid play with other children,
to find spaces of her own,
to make daisy chains.

But she is joining the world
one stem to another,
holding them delicately
so as not to hurt the fragile partitions
of their yellow heads, pressing them
through moist stems, links in a chain of light
white-yellow-green
            white-yellow-green
                        white-yellow-green

Naming fire

The man talked in Welsh, long-haired, loose-belted,
talked in Welsh as if we might remember it,
we simply, for centuries, had not been trying.
Then he took two tinders and struck them

so sparks leapt and shrunk back to stone.
Caraig he said, showing the child
the smouldering coals spreading honey light
as if to say: *this is how we do it.*

I was sure the word he showed was fire,
what he made with the flints, how they struck
and sparked and leapt through the long tongues of time
into a fire forged from word –

but it was my misunderstanding and it was
the making he named, *caraig* to *crag* to *stone,*
how time transforms, how cold leads to heat,
and how heat comes back to stone.

School photo

The Jewish school, Warsaw, 1929

In the school photo, four rows of children,
boys in white shirts, smiling, smirking, grimacing,
the girls in their tunics with box necks,
neat white collars, preparing for their futures –

still-faced that minute in the lens eye, in between
the fidgeting, failing to sit up straight, pulling
faces, sticking out a tongue, trying to make
teacher laugh, and in the bottom row on the left

there he is, my young-boy father, his face sweet
with life as yet unspent, his dark eyes staring
intensely at the viewer, who knows him now
more than he knows himself – how the shy

half-smile, the straining forward towards the camera,
the black hair cut straight above his eyes,
hold the story of the flight to come, the healer
he is to be, the spouse, the father, not yet known.

The moment is held here, *click*,
before they all, row by row, child by child,
scatter with playground shouts, tugs of war,
hide-and-seek, empty rooms.

The last cinema before flight

Warsaw, 1938

One day, not knowing why,
you were locked out of school,
found another thing to do –
daytime cinema, delicious truancy,
sitting in the dark in the back row
beside a satchel and a Polish grammar.

You did not know this was the limbo
of leaving, daytime darkness, a paring
of life to black and white, how it started
separations – the horse's pull
on the street carriage, the boy you sat beside
in the school photo.

Now you are in a
cocoon of camera dark, the director
in his box of light, the crackle
of figures flickering in and out of shadow,
the silent mime.

It divided the world
in two: that which had come to pass,
and that which was still to come,
the reel of memory with its repeated moves,
remembered scenes clicking off and on,

and that last scene
when they walk into the horizon
and you can only imagine.

Divided city

The new child came as pale survivor
of a split city, and because I saw
the wall in him, how it peeled
and quartered the heart

I became his words: *hello - goodbye*
playtime dinner time
time for home

as he felt for them
in the limbo land
amongst the fixity of desks
the day's white noise
I am Turkey
I am Turkish

holding memories hotly in his fist
like a shell, its memory of sea
and I, the other side,
waving, asking him to leap.

not a poem

I promised you
there would be
no more poems
about you,

those silly shapes
made by grown-ups,
for no good reason
at all.

They are not transformers,
like your metal cars –
they don't sing
like Michael Jackson,

they would not win
a talent competition,
you can't fly them
like a Chinese kite,

ride them like a dodgem car,
they don't taste like
chocolate twizzlers, or do
magic tricks with rabbits

and paper bags. The words
do not stick on the ceiling
or make rude noises
like fart balloons.

They have, quite simply,
no point at all. So this
is not a poem, and
just as I promised, this

is not about you at all.

I am the sum of my libraries

Here is the children's library I loved –
travelling bears, secret fives,
middle earths, flying cars,
tin men, talking dogs –

and here the school library, where girls and boys
exchanged hopeless glances, like aliens
from separate stars, testing their French,
feeling their blood leap

and here the fearsome shelves of the University,
interminable forests you can only traverse
alone, like birth,
in the company of former souls.

I am the sum of my libraries,
the ways they travel, the trees they plant.
The trails are laid with leaves, some to hold
like badges, others like a map of veins,
the way blood moves.

They have never ceased their whispering,
words behind words, waiting to be heard.

Clock without hands, Paignton Pier

I am a handless clock not
fulfilling life's mission,
treadmill of time.
I look out now with my face

round as the moon and my view,
like the rushing of sea, the bracing
of wind, the gull's wake over summer,
is a delicious failure of expectations.

I am unemployed, a guesswork,
the opposite of myself.

Beside me, like a row of sunflowers,
the beach-hut faces. You ask of them
what you dream of behind painted doors –

yourself as a child
in red-spotted swimsuit,
bucket in fist, spade
full of damp sand, standing there

as if time had stopped.

Find the One

the cobweb of outlawed lanes,
the outside-walls I loved, where gypsies
and rough-smoking exiles lived –

I remember them with absolute clarity
as if they were long-loved fairytales
or favourite shoes –

or think I do,

because the streets have picked themselves up,
shuffled themselves around, shaken up the habitual
with their easy chains of thought,
asked me to rethink, choose a substitute
for the memory I am trying to reach.

Again and again the turnings
do not lead to my young-girl street,
no house is quite the one,
the windows, shutters,
faded paint on the iron gate –

something is slipping away –
and though my footsteps begin
to resign themselves to a house
nearly the same, a street almost there,

my heart is unsatisfied.
There can be no substitutes.
It is not enough to be almost there.
Find the one, the very one.

House in my prime

I returned to the house of my prime,
to see if I was in.
All the signs were there, the shutters
rolled up to let in the summer light,
as I used to do –

the gate its same battered shade of green,
with the locked box behind
that I had opened daily with such leaps of hope,
awaiting letters from home,
with a small key that seemed so inconsequential,
so easy to break.

Through the iron gate I could see the single step
to the green front door, where once I slid
and concussed myself on the hardened ice,
and beyond that the fig tree where cats had prowled
with tiger-eyes surveying the tall grass for
the movement of mice.

Yes, it had its times of pure frost
when it was an island on the frozen lake,
and times where it was the only spot of cool
in a baking plate of sun. It was the house
of my prime, when I was flush with
vines and hopes, and growing what I was.

Now it stands between my life
and the life of someone else I do not know
the other side of the holding walls,
dividing us so they on the inside, I on the outside
do not see our common memory –
how much we are joined.

The shutter maker

I watch the shutter maker at the kitchen table
thread the wood slat by slat.

Hour by hour his fingers dance
between thread and wood.

Yes, I am eighty, he says,
and the last man of my craft.

All afternoon I hear the *click click*
like castanets, of the slats joining,

falling in wooden drapes over the table,
until, when all the labour is done

he clicks the shutters closed,
and the slats drop into a perfect fall.

He threads his way home
past the pink church, through the old quarter,

across the vineyards to the concrete gash
where the new-build windows stand

in naked glare, their eyes lined
with aluminium strips,

blinds bright with painted birds,
the occasional splash of a fabric flower.

This measured day, striped now
with light, the musk of warm wood,

is your work of art, last man of your craft,
your signature is here, and we will remember.

Budapest balcony

The balcony has always eavesdropped
on the street. When the people inside
were playing chess or attending to patients
or storing tins of beans against the hunger,

it poked its iron ear out into the street
and played the innocent with its pots of basil
and live shoots of thyme. But really
it heard how the coffee shop rolled up
its metal blinds and enticed the early workers

rushing to their places of tedious repetition
in office buildings, neighbours learned of one another
as they met for the first time by the shared front door,
young men flocked to Freedom Square
flying flags with gutted hearts

and came back at night draped limp
over the shoulders of the living, the doctor
who lived in the upstairs room on the pavement
weeping, as soldiers paced by
with buttons shining like chocolate coins,

The balcony has always eavesdropped on the street,
its iron ear hearing all that passes,
playing the innocent with its pots of basil,
its live shoots of thyme.

Bronze shoes along the Danube

Here is a smart laced pair
in brown lived-in leather that bent
to his foot and the many ways it walked him.
singer, pianist, music-hall star.

and a pert black pair of mules
with a neat heel and square toes
that must have teamed
with a nipped-in jacket and skirt
as she made brisk passage
between safe houses.
vintner, knew every vintage with a single sniff.

A pair of sturdy peasant boots
pulled on in dead dark mornings
with hands large enough to calm chickens
or birth a calf, the missing laces
letting the leather fall loose
for the last walk.
chicken farmer, chickens koshered and trief.

A pair of baby boots
with embroidered daisies,
red laces untied
ready for toes to spread after their
warm uncurling from sleep.
first child, so long awaited.

They are kicked along the front
any-old-how, some separated from their mate
in small migrations.
The river tries to cleanse itself
again and again, in its longing to survive.

but its memory rebirths here.
What is there becomes the shape
of what is not there, its refusal to forget
cast in bronze, their going, their failure to come back.

Shabbat in Budapest

The cantor faced his listeners like a stranger
weeping on our shoulder in a crowded place
unpacking his song without stop or shame.

Then we turned and saw, carved in marble
like skeins of flaxen hair, names of the quiet ones
who planned discreet and lawful lives
in neighbouring courtyards, whose last goal
amongst the kosher kitchens, was heroic,
or unheroic, or indeed collective death
of any kind –

rows of them
chipped precisely into stone
columns of them
constellations of them
a myriad of pale stars
tapped in by the stonemason
a whole weeping cavalcade
of fallen chips.

We sang

suddenly, for them,
for the protests that never marched
the roofs that never sheltered
the wakes that never mourned

for the silenced voices
blown to prayer

What have they done to the land?

Oahu, Hawaii

It was a land open to the sea
on all sides, and in the round
the light came in, luminous,
like a window in its transparency
to another side, its mountains
serrating the sky, ringed
by bands of gold, the soft floor
between land and sea.

The land then was the body of gods,
their hair stroked like banyan trees,
their hearts bursting with fire.

Then the land was stolen,
cut into pieces like a patchwork,
sold to the highest bidders, the gods
shorn of their hair, their mouths
stopped with concrete, their stories
scattered on the buried land.

Where is the light now?
Where is the heart of the gods?
What have they done to the land?

Drought

Orgiva, Spain

The sun has cornered us
holed us into white space
pours burning oil over white walls
and shoots its tiny needles.

It has invaded the air
and the figs that face it
fall smashed and steaming
in its path.

You have occupied the land,
burning pathways to each village,
valley and villa, and not a creature
that lives, not a panting goat,
souring vine, parched river,
escapes your march.

The cows are showing sharp
shoulder bones, scrabbling
in the balding grass for food.
They are the gaunt ghosts
of our own pain, swaddled like us
in a moist sheath of sweat.

The fans murmur hopelessly,
lifting limp puffs of air,
and from the hedges cicadas,
like invisible warriors,
cry out in constant, cackling chorus.

There is no escape from our escalation
of heat, the way we have fuelled our own
fires, laid out all that we love
  — burnt offerings to a furious god.

Arizona sun

The terrain is something to read
like a gecko face, scaled and pitted,
warts sprouting cactus spines.

It is a great happening
the sky,
it is a declaration,
huge
we hadn't known
how huge it could be.

It breaks out wherever there is a chance to see
and in each place
rocks tipped and scattered
a ransack of a rockscape
a crazy creation workshop
with unmade faces, monuments

but now nothing answers back
not a bird not a howl
not a single footstep –

it has nuded itself of anything that lives,
it has left itself
the shapes of things that moved
the carved sockets of things that saw.

All that is alive springs needles,
cacti knobs, spiked aureoles of thorn

and we hurry away
before the sky escapes
and finds us

Dance-charm

Santiago, Chile

I am watching the people dancing to the band,
to the clapping started up in the crowd. –

They jump into the circle,
men in wide-brimmed hats,
girls with swinging ponytails,

swaying and winding with and between,
in and out of the music, some
with a new face picked from the crowd,
others with lifelong loves, or soon-to-be,

and in the *clack tarakata* of the beat
I hear
        come you dance
and I say
        no no I don't know the steps
and he persists
        yes yes you dance!

and thrusts into my hand
a white handkerchief of dance-surrender

so I leap into the circle, hair and
handkerchief blown here, there,
       kirakaraka kirakaraka
become the thread, winding like them
in and between and with and in and out

and all my clutter and ghosts
leave the circle, charmed to dust,
and as they leave the circle,
they cannot help but smile.

that bright fandango

Somewhere in a mistaken skip
is my address book, a lost heart
known only to itself.

There is no ritual for mourning
its scored-out places in coloured pens,
pasted cards, dead heads of names and numbers

that were an Aladdin's cave
of half-lived loves and faded friends.
The tangle of loose ends,

sloping tails and tines,
unlocked secret codes,
a lottery of hopes –

all that bright fandango
that was a life
thrown into the hinterland of things

where lost objects float
waiting for us to arrive.

Butterfly amongst grapes

How grapes are hard at the core,
the seed at the start of it blooming out
fleshy, shining globes
covered with papal purple
papery skin, clusters of sticky twins.

How butterflies are another way
to be alive — wrapped and hanging
unborn inside a case, encouraged
by sun, how you drop
slowly, empty out, leave behind,

transmitted into harsh air —
the stripe, the spot, paper thinness,
the not-quite-sound of the flap,
the whirr, as the aerial of summer
draws to the sweetness of fruits,

in this wink of time
passing from life to life,
shape to shape, the different ways
it is possible to be alive.

Turbulence

What if all this circling in the air
never stopped
and this stranger caught short in shock
was the last to sit alongside,
and the last sweat to break
was fear.

What if all the trawling of empty space
came to this,
and the shiver of a new moon
was the closing scene.

We are all now writing our last poems,
from one line home
to epics of self-confession,
hoping it's like falling downstairs,

that we will dust ourselves off, and feeling
faintly ridiculous, no more than this,
walk through sliding doors to our destination,
try the ground for movement, find it solid.

Rolling now against the whiteout,
the steel wings rearing and bucking –
we are eggs in a mixing bowl
afraid of breaking, afraid of spilling
our pinpoints of gold.

It is this great body of steel
we pray to.
The clouds refuse to deliver
any other god but this.

Seeing Mount Fuji

Here the viewing window had no view,
it had a shroud of mist that promised
the absence of view and what it might have been
had the absence been filled.

So we walked past expecting nothing, thinking
we would have the pictures we draw
inside our minds, and were unprepared for the sky's
new display, its sudden glorious invitation, its sudden
yes

as if a veil had lifted into a secret chamber
showing the inside workings of a cosmic mind,
the way it thought symmetry, planned for solid,
capped its peaks with powderings to show
the nature of cold, of climates, the varying
of height to depth, what would happen to rock
if, anchored to the planet, it longed to fly.

We shriek with joy, aghast at the giant,
how his heaving into view makes a crack in the sky,
breaks open the heavens,
and we hold on to him, Fuji-san,
like a snowflake translating into vapour,
or knowledge itself bursting into sense
before fading, becoming memory.

is a gateway

to a red wooden temple, brilliantly lit,

is a gateway
to a row of flat bells on a wooden beam with heavy ropes inviting pulling,

is a gateway
to a row of steps leading to a golden tiger under a red canopy

is a gateway
to a wooden hut where a calligrapher is bent over a fine brush
painting kanji delicately

is a gateway
to a wooden platform with a stone pagoda and a carved fox climbing
to meet it

is a gateway
to steep steps mounting a hill

is a gateway
to a five-tiered pagoda in stone with open arch gathering rainwater

is a gateway
to a row of lanterns hanging in trees marked with kanji to the wood gods

is a gateway
to a break in the trees gathering bright red leaf-fall on a pea-soup pond

is a gateway
to an archway like a giant red moon on its back growing black as the
day darkens

is a gateway
to a corridor of red pillars alongside a stream

is a gateway
to a corridor of red pillars turning a corner

is a gateway
to a corridor of red pillars leading to a lone bell above a stone shrine
and a cat disturbed from sleep

is a gateway
to a corridor of red pillars winding into the woods disappearing to a
point,

is a gateway

Tea-ceremony

To pass the threshold you must
stoop low, discarding swords,

then, disarmed, join
the space between inner and outer,

the gardens partly screened,
partly revealed, stone beside leaf, falling water

against still. It is a place
where nothing is an accident; not the joining

of mats, the holding of bowls, the imitating
of leaves; and she kneels, bows to tea,

thanking it for its travel from tree to leaf
to powder; offers it the kettle,

its belly warmed on the sunken hob,
poured into two china cups, then,

with a ladle smoothed by
the precision of cloth she stirs the mix

into a broth, two cups, for each guest
one. *But will you not drink too?* I ask.

She stands, moves behind the screen,
some mark has split the ritual in two,

returns, third cup in her hand.
I cannot drink unless I am invited, she says.

You are very elegant to ask.
We drink, the three of us, quietly,

savouring how leaves are ground to a paste
and hurried into froth, how slow grown

and how nursed into life.
Elegance, I am glad it found me.

The orange-lemon

The temple is a place of remembrance, healing the join
between life and death, and we share green tea
whisked into pea-soup, and cake the fineness of
sacred wafer. Even the porcelain that holds them
is a hymn to the seasons, delicate as the leaves
burned by autumn, and we are seated low
alongside the sunken kettle, where ground is,
where tatami mesh together.

You may meet my wife, he says, with his robes
wrapped around him, cross-legged on the tatami mats
that are the floor's plaited skin.
But you are a Buddhist monk? I think. *How can that be?*
Because I do not know enough, and I do not know
what is and what can be, he stands up to fetch her,
brings her in by the hand from behind the sliding screen.
We sit together and explain how each one of us,

is not what we seem. And then the monk leads us
into the garden he tends, with its stone memorials
and the path between them, and reaches into the bunchy
arms of the tree with a pole and clips a fruit
with its flirtation of leaves, and brings it down to meet us.
It has both the tartness of a lemon, and the sweetness
of an orange: the pale ovalness of the one,
and the bunchy roundness of the other.

Cut it in two, he says, *and put half in the bath.*
And should I eat the other half? I think
or half and half; making flesh
into fruit, taste into scent, other into other.
Or should it be none of these
as you give me no answer. Or is it this.
It is an orange-lemon.
It is what it is to be opposite.

Onsen

Hot water spring, Kyoto

Stepping into the hot spring
oh you must groan with the bliss
of it, how water makes a space
for you, meets your blood halfway,
a heat exactly where the blood is,
holds you like plankton, without
edge or weight, the water in you
singing to itself, the you in water
recognising itself, bringing you home.

Swimming deeper

I used to crash on the surface
like a speedboat,
pushing out elbows and knees
so that the whole water face
crumpled and scattered.

Then you said,
swim deeper, do the stretching
deep below the surface

and I moved lower into it,
where sounds were darker
and pulled like a magnet
and slid my hands between the layers

and saw how the wind
rolled the walnut tree
over the surface and all its
elbow angles melted
into liquid velvet.

Swim deeper and feel yourself
where push and pull meet,
in between the two.

Saving a ladybird

Today I saved a ladybird
in the swimming pool,
its two spots folded flat
on the still killing wave.

I was a nobbled pink island,
hoving up from the hopeless depths,
erupting and lifting it
onto dry beach

and it clung to me like a swimmer,
crawling shipwrecked onto sand
and ran, its legs like tiny hairs,
exploring its new terrain –

the way life is saved,
or snatched on a whim,
the way its wings unwrap,
spread the air with their tiny spots,

Strand

The seagulls are lined up in the sand
facing into the wind to steady them

staring into the wind with a hostile gaze
like school teachers shaming unruly boys.

Their beaks are pinched shut in shock
and they will not move, the wind

has shocked them into silence
pinned their feathers flat, all their bustle

stilled by gripping
the task of holding on

but for one, trying it on, wheeling up,
her wings turn inside out, batter her backwards.

The others roll a sideways eye
pretend to be stone,

slate-grey winter gods
waiting for time to set them free.

Dartmoor standing stones

Time has not finished here,
sculpting stone with sand-carrying
wind, chiselling ruts with frozen rain.

Time moves slowly,
cools and harries new angles,
a company of elders, polished

by sleet and travellers' hands,
their robes of stone soothed into
leaning pyramids, baby tors,

they lift needle heads to the moor,
their layers of micro-life
moving on the face of their fixed earth.

On falling into the River Thames
disembarking from our narrowboat

When I felt my foot slide
there was no stopping it, an
unwilling flamenco into the
river's black slosh, and then,

a boot, a knee, another one of each,
crumbling into icy beads of shock,
the river's, mine, as all of us
rush to baptism.

I grab for land, all the day's
paraphernalia and I in fatal
connection, crashing

from air to water, where
quiet perch glide slowly past,
coming in from another element.

My wooden men

Site of the defunct Oxford to Witney railway line

Following the wharf stream past the allotments
over the road and through the iron gate

I come across the wooden men,
chunky and life-size –

you can hug them and feel the heft of them,
worry how their flat caps fare in the rain.

They are resting
by the side of the railway line they had dug,

and you know their work was meant to usher something in –
the to and fro of labour and life,

the chain of villages joined up like DNA.
But the line has gone, stripped back

to an indent through the field, its arrow of hope
camouflaged in tall grass.

I feel a kind of kinship between us,
the solidness of their kind wooden bones ...

No need to worry now, I say.
We are going home.

Visiting Dylan

Dylan Thomas's house, Laugharne

I came as a pilgrim
to the winter house
the rain blowing upwards from the sea,
downwards from the swollen grey sky

and found the green door open
walked through into the homeliness
with its dung brown walls, spiney chairs,
the pimply desk, the memory of cigarette butts,

sat at the living room table
and watched your sea through the window
lashing up to the soaked terrace

and wondered if it was I
who had been there always
and you just passing through

how I had found a space between the bottles
and butts and unwashed cups to meet you
and to meet me coming back from meeting you

Hôtel-Dieu-Saint-Esprit, Arles

Bed 41: Vincent Van Gogh

They brought the new patient in,
so pale his veins were veiled blue
as if frozen still in his nightmare,
and I saw his eyes, tunnels
into the centre of nothing,
where he floated, watching himself there,

spiralling down. I saw it all
in the first moment, his head tight
between his two hands,
strong and brown as a farmer's,
wild, bright things held out
like rich strangers in a hungry land.

He knew the irises in the garden;
they bowed to him like the faces of friends,
purple, red, orange,
while we floated meaningless,
with medicine and meals on metal trays,
calling him in from another world.

Meeting the Green Man

Lud's Church, Gradbach

At first he leads your eye down
where your foot treads in bleeding mulch
or up the stone ascension of steps,
to chandeliers of beech lit with autumn,
corridors narrowing to a needle of light.
He teases you with invisible angles,
cul-de-sac chapels where stone totems
rear moss-shaggy heads, petrified guests
beat their stone heads against jagged wall,
and in the day-dark, seats of stone
await you in sunken inglenooks –

and you are in the abandoned mansion
of an absent lord, travelling like an innocent
thinking yourself alone –

                                        and then you see him,
the presiding god, his features
prising themselves from the crevices,
his nose the button of a child you know,
his eyes shadowed and overhung
from a millennium of beating by wind and snow,
his lips a silenced fissure through stone.

Are you evil giant or trapped prophet,
mindful god or beheaded knight,
bursting from stone or petrified from flesh,
written in stone or the face-in-my-mind?

Stay awhile, he says.
Stay awhile and hear me.
Stay awhile and hear what I have to say –

What I would like to say

What I'd like to say to the nay-sayers is
how would it be if yours were not the only world
it were possible to inhabit,
if the leaps you said could not be made,
were made.

What if you slipped the skins that seal you,
leaving behind the bright
abandoned husk. It can be done.
Cobras do, cabbage whites do.

What if we are both wrong, I about you,
you about me, and that where I must go
is a leap
from knowing to not knowing, and you
must make the same leap too –

both of us, being brave,
from thinking we are right,
to wondering if we are wrong –

from holding a stone
to holding a question about space –
how it has evolved to be this.

Icescape

Water moves like the blood in us,
holding its movement up to be seen,
its angers, its strange calms —

mirror of us, how it lets all go,
breaking out of boundaries
in its run for life

or, frozen, holds itself
trapped in patterns,
its light through veins

a coloured map of hopes —
the way ice goes nowhere,
holds its breath, never arrives.

Snowscape

It is a white in us, in our secret place we are this,
this white.

It has the quiet of recognition, as if it's a place
we struggle to remember –

how it was before sound separated into words,
when we moved like astronauts slowly,
without gravity,

when colours were just presence or absence of light,
when we were a blank page, a beginning.

Our first place,
                    it was white.

Museum for the blind

It is very dark here, even for the blind
and it is they who lead,
seeing with their hands,
teaching us to do so.

I am learning how it is to be
slow, very slow, letting touch
go first, controlling the way
panic might make mistakes

fail to feel the edge
of a step, the sharp solid
of a table corner.

Touch is making shapes
in the darkroom of the mind.
Is the table red?
Is the sky still slate, or grey,

or sometimes blue?
Do I remember colour?
Can I make sculpture
by feeling the curve of a marble arm,
the cold curls of David's head?

Is it like this,
when eyes have finished
their service to the outside world,
and all its colour
is made by the mind,
by its private longing for light?

Cleaning the wall

The old lady in the green dress
wants to sit on the promenade wall.

The old man who walks by her side
takes out a paper tissue

folds it very small
and with it he wipes the surface,

scrubs it so the dust
feathers up from the stone,

the dead cells of children's sandals
specks of sand and ice cream cones

pollen dropped from ancient hibiscus
the staining stamens of lilies

the milky spit of seagulls,
dust feathering down

from the Moors' white tower.
When the old man

has cleaned the wall
the old lady sits down.

He stands beside her,
holding her stick, he

who would not let the winds of heaven
visit her face too roughly

and she, in the *chariot of burnished gold*
that is his heart.

Italicised words with thanks to Shakespeare.

Father and child cross the road

I don't know on which day
it changed:
I, tightly hemmed
beside you, learning about the road,
about looking from right to left,
learning to imagine
beyond the brow of hills, how
the pushing head of lights could leap
snarling from any turn,
you teaching me the right moment
to cross from shore to shore

to the day when it changed around

and it was I holding you tightly hemmed,
I measuring the speed between lights,
preparing for their dazzle, planning for
the brows of hills, moving you into safe terrain,
the snarling eyes of cars prowling
the dark strip, separating safety
from safety, I waiting for a pause
in the flow, the right moment
to guide you gently from shore to shore.

Bay View café

For a week you had been anchored to the drips,
your theatre the stilled lives around you
stopped in their tracks, and your view,

framed in the far window, the edge
of a shaking tree, the jagged corner of a roof
and an occasional shadow of birdwing like a message

from the free world. And then the liberation, –
when you walked slowly to see how steps felt,
how it was to be upright, how it was

to find the café in the hospital lobby,
choose the softest seat, ask for a latte,
and then change your mind, stand up,

thread your way past tables and chairs
to the whole-wall window and stand there,
facing the spread sea,

the sudden infinity.
The café is called Bay View, you said,
And it is.
It is.

These last days

1.
The ambulance meets a point in time
where outside it breaks sound, screaming
through the streets, but inside
it runs slow and cold as a drain.
We drape the padded coat over you,
keep talking about journeys, planes and cars and
how we travel these days, and then
I find my furry hat and put it on your head,
let the warm rim circle you.

As you lie propped on pillows
you say
I do not groan for pain
but for relief, and when I walk
I see small creatures, animals or
small children, I take care
not to bump them, but as I do,
I understand they are not there at all,
but lining my own mind.

You start at the sound of your childhood name,
Miecik. Your DNA leaps at the memory.
It is what we share.

We are not sure now what it is you know,
as we circle you, sit beside you,
stroke your head, whisper your name.
You take time for your journey,
your eyes searching above,
beyond us, as if it is something else you see.

The bear-blanket you chose for warmth
is falling, rising, falling, rising.
It has come to this.
You are breathing and we are glad.

A smile starts across your cheeks,
but it has left its starting place,
and we will not see its end
though it seems, by its greeting,
that others might. I fear
my envy. They
have the quick of you and we
the perfectly crafted shell
of where you lived.

I pick up the traces,
press them into my heart –
all its emptied spaces.

Great-aunt Esther

She arrived one night,
from howling plains of nameless land,
silver forests, harsh black nights
on a boat's icy deck, to the door,
the beacon of the doorbell –
the amazement of a new aunt.

In our kitchen I spun around her,
she making strudel on the kitchen table,
I sitting under it like the house cat
singing invented songs, and she
songs with words from her other land,
and I tasted the sweet dough,
the sweetness of apples on a wooden spoon.

She must have sat in the upright chair
making the cloth to cover bread,
each poppyseed sewn in, seed by seed,
the bread edged in gold thread, letters
picked out in black, wishing us peace.

Then one day great-aunt
was snatched into the strange cave
of an uncle. People said
what a chance, so late in life,
how lucky, at last.

Great-aunt disappeared
to his country, ringed with wire,
became a wife in headscarf,
shaved head and borrowed daughters,
baked dough with no history,
stilled by strange words,
forelocks and prayer, uncle
rocking, eyes closed
in black gowns, in fancy dress.

I think of her crossing the sea
and arriving, finding the doorbell
in the darkness, and the door opening,
the cries of joy, the words, the words,
and then, I think of her stepping inside
and staying there, with us,
staying in the warmth.

Day of Atonement

We are sitting closely
around the top corner of the table
formally dressed for the new year,
its candles lit and ready with its bowls
anticipating soup, for the breaking
of the fast.

It is the first year you have been
too short of breath to join the congregation
so we are watching the service,
beamed onto a tablet propped against a plate,

and it takes us right onto the platform,
the rabbi in white shawl singing
for the end of day. The shofar moans
its last held breath that marks
the closure of prayers, and the last signing
in the book of life.

You listen to it, with your ear
pressed against the tablet,
and sometimes you fall asleep, your chin
dropped down into your chest,
your eyelids flickering

and I sit beside you, as I never could before,
and stroke your hair, your soft silver hair,
waiting for you to wake up.

One sun, one moon

While we see the moon on its back,
pink light spilling from sky,
long afternoon shadows,
the red flash of the honeycreeper,

on the other side of the world
it is winter, with the moon
up-ended, cheese-pared, light
draining daily into a sink of dark.

Once they thought the planet was
flat, that we all shared the same
seasons, daybreaks, changes of light.

It was a failure of imagination
believing the edge was an ending,
an absence of empathy.

When one side is in bursting spring,
on the other side all the leaves
are shedding, and earth is returning
to where it began.

Oversteps Books Ltd

The Oversteps list includes books by the following poets:

David Grubb, Giles Goodland, Alex Smith, Will Daunt, Patricia Bishop, Christopher Cook, Jan Farquarson, Charles Hadfield, Mandy Pannett, Doris Hulme, James Cole, Helen Kitson, Bill Headdon, Avril Bruton, Marianne Larsen, Anne Lewis-Smith, Mary Maher, Genista Lewes, Miriam Darlington, Anne Born, Glen Phillips, Rebecca Gethin, W H Petty, Melanie Penycate, Andrew Nightingale, Caroline Carver, John Stuart, Rose Cook, Jenny Hope, Hilary Elfick, Anne Stewart, Oz Hardwick, Terry Gifford, Michael Swan, Maggie Butt, Anthony Watts, Robert Stein, Graham High, Ross Cogan, Ann Kelley, Diane Tang, R V Bailey, John Daniel, Alwyn Marriage, Kathleen Kummer, Jean Atkin, Charles Bennett, Elisabeth Rowe, Marie Marshall, Ken Head, Robert Cole, Cora Greenhill, John Torrance, Michael Bayley, Christopher North, Simon Richey, Lynn Roberts, Sue Davies, Mark Totterdell, Michael Thomas, Ann Segrave, Helen Overell, Rose Flint, Denise Bennett, James Turner, Sue Boyle, Jane Spiro, Jennie Osborne, John Daniel, Janet Loverseed, Wendy Klein, Sally Festing, Angela Stoner, Simon Williams, Susan Taylor, Richard Skinner, Fokkina McDonnell, Joan McGavin, David Broadbridge, Sue Proffitt, Christine Whittemore, A C Clarke, Ian Royce Chamberlain, Melanie Branton, Denise McSheehy and Rebecca Bilkau.

For details of all these books, information about Oversteps and up-to-date news, please look at our website and blog:

www.overstepsbooks.com
http://overstepsbooks.wordpress.com